The Unspeakable Scot

Clifford Hanley

CLIFFORD HANLEY, a native and resident Glaswegian, started his working life in journalism and still contributes regularly to several newspapers, but moved into the theatre, radio and television, both as a writer and performer. His published books include *Dancing in the Streets, Love from Everybody, The Taste of Too Much, A Skinful of Scotch, The Redhaired Bitch* and *The Hot Month*; and (as Henry Calvin) *The System, The DNA Business, The Italian Gadget, Miranda Must Die, It's Different Abroad, The Chosen Instrument, The Poison Chasers* and *Take Two Popes*.

Song lyrics, mostly written for Scottish musical shows, include 'Scotland the Brave', 'Wachlin' Hame', 'The Glasgow Underground', 'Jock Mackay' and 'The Noo'.

Cover illustration by John Mackay

THE
UNSPEAKABLE
SCOT

Clifford Hanley

Illustrated by John Mackay

WILLIAM BLACKWOOD

First published in 1977 by
William Blackwood & Sons Ltd
32 Thistle Street
Edinburgh EH2 1HA
Scotland

Reprinted 1979
Reprinted 1981

ISBN 0 85158 120 X
Printed by William Blackwood & Sons Ltd

Contents

INVASION—THE STAPLE DIET Scotland is a small country, occupying the northern portion of the main island of Great Britain. Its total area is about 30,000 square miles, and its population is around five million. In the global scheme of things it is not very important. But like many small countries it is a highly particular place, and outsiders recognise that the Scots are a highly particular people.

Like other people of small nations, they are touchy. If an innocent outsider fails to recognise their particularity—if he assumes for instance that the Scots are a branch of the English—some of them are capable of taking offence.

The innocent outsider may be forgiven, because Scotland is geographically joined to England and Wales; the Scots speak and read the English language, they share the monarchy and other important institutions like the taxation system.

The Scottish Parliament was merged into the English Parliament in 1707, and there are respectable historians who declare that Scotland was never a nation in any real sense even before then. Other Scots take offence at this statement. Many Scots take offence regularly at nearly anything. If there is such a thing as a national trait, taking offence is a Scottish national trait.

Today, the peculiar Scottish character, as seen from outside, is often a stereotype compounded of tartan, whisky, stinginess and a comic dialect composed of gutturals and rolling Rs. There is something in it. Tartan, whisky, stinginess and strange dialects are to be found in Scotland. However, so also are sober clothes, sober habits, generosity and good plain speech. As with all national groups, the Scots are a complex picture.

. . . taking offence is a Scottish national trait

They are, most people find, quite likeable, and worth study and understanding.

We may logically begin with the history, which is fully as violent and confusing as that of ordinary people.

In the ice ages, Scotland had and was ice, punctuated by mountain peaks and unseen by man. The ice gave way to great forests, which were in turn ground away by new ice before men came, and new forests grew.

The first inhabitants lived near the coasts, sheltered in caves, fished and hunted and used stone implements. We know very little about them, except that their descendants improved and crept into the Bronze Age. They were small men with long heads, and their descendants may be recognised today at any football match.

They were probably helped up the technological ladder by invasions from mainland Europe, which included the Beaker People, who buried their dead in huge circular graves and included with them a tall earthen vessel by which we know them.

By the time the Romans came to North Britain, the scene was quite complicated. Roman observers called some of the natives Picts, or painted people, from the habit of painting their bodies with woad. Personally, I have always regarded this tale with Scottish irreverence, because the Scottish climate is rarely warm enough to encourage nudity. It is just as likely that the impoverished aborigines had only one set of clothes, and when that was in the wash they had to run about the mountains trying to keep warm. Well might they look blue.

In any case, the Picts, and Pictish culture, were on their way out as a separate phenomenon. The western islands of Europe were already infiltrated by Celtic tribes—Goidels, Brythons and Belgae—who had drifted across the Continent until they reached the edge of the world. By the time the Romans arrived, the Britons were masters, and their language was the language of Britain. It was a tongue related to modern Welsh.

Invasion was to be the staple diet of Scotland. It seems strange that anyone should covet such an inhospitable land, but men are driven by strange demons.

Rome was content with its conquest of England early in the Christian era, but in A.D. 80 Julius Agricola drove north and overran southern Scotland as far as Perthshire, with sizeable losses on both sides. The Britons of the time were less a nation than a group of squabbling tribes, but they united well enough against the invaders before they were broken. And during the next few decades they made life miserable for the army of occupation.

In fact, North Britain—Scotland—was occupied rather than conquered. In A.D. 140 the Emperor Antoninus Pius sent fresh legions to consolidate the outpost. The commander, Lollius Urbicus, joined up a line of deserted forts, left by Agricola, with a ten-foot-high wall running across the country from the River Forth to the River Clyde. It was splendid and authoritative, and little scraps of it are still to be found; but it was too far from Rome. In a few decades the rebellious locals had wearied the Empire and Rome's Scottish adventure was over.

A small legend remains, that Pontius Pilate was born in Perthshire while his father was engaged in that glum campaign. Like much of Scotland's history, the tale is both fascinating and irrelevant.

The country was plagued by Saxon pirates, and by the Scots. The very name Scot is an Irish importation. Later there were incursions by the Vikings, who became masters of the Hebrides, parts of the western mainland of Scotland, and the Isle of Man. Their occupation came to an end after the Scottish king Alexander scored an indecisive victory over them at the Battle of Largs in 1263. But it isn't easy to decide how much anybody ruled anybody. The Romans never really controlled the north of Scotland, and when the Norsemen were driven out, as the historian Robert Mackie sums up, 'so Kintyre and the Hebrides at last formed part of the kingdom of Scotland. It made very little difference to the Islesmen; hitherto they had disobeyed the King of Norway; now they disobeyed the King of Scots'.

Disobedience to powers and principalities is a notice-

4

able element in the Scottish character, with a long and respectable history.

It is interesting that the prolonged Norwegian occupation of the west and the islands has left no effect on the language, except for a few place-names. They have left other traces, however. Today, there is no 'typical' Scot. There are several.

. . . there is no 'typical' Scot. There are several

There is that low-slung, long-headed throwback to the Picts, whose strain is reinforced by incursions from Ireland, which also had its Picts in the old times. Irish legend calls the type the little black men. At the same time we have the massive Highlander, blond or fiery red, with Norse blood in his big frame.

And here and there you may find other dark, sallow people who may well date from the Spanish Armada, which abandoned more than one ship off the west of Scotland.

YE HIGHLANDS AND YE LOWLANDS   All the same, is Scotland unique or peculiar to itself? The Scot who senses its uniqueness and tries to isolate it may be in danger of seeing in blinkers, and this danger may be illustrated on the most ordinary level. Some years ago a sociologist working on children's games compiled a radio programme in which he revealed that many of these games are universal, except for one particular ritual found only in the Loop district of Chicago.

As he went on to describe the rules of this game, I realised that he was talking about hunch-cuddy-hunch, a ludicrous activity common to my own tenement childhood in Glasgow.

It is a futile exercise beloved of children, and requires a wall. The chosen champion bends and presses his hands against the wall, to represent a horse (cuddy is the Lowland Scots word for a horse). Another child leaps astride him, then another, and another, and the point of the game is to support the maximum number of bodies before collapsing.

Like many of the best things in life, it is unprofitable. But I had imagined that it was unique and peculiar to Glasgow, while the sociologist had fancied it existed nowhere but in Chicago. I cite this little story to remind myself that when I notice something totally Scottish, it may also be Chinese or Bolivian. We all imagine we are something special.

All the same, I do find the Scots peculiar and par- ticular. And considering how few they are, they come in an astonishing variety.

(1) The clan—a family business One group contains the Highlanders, or Gaels. They are imagined by some people to be the typical Scots, but in fact they are a minority of a few hundred thousand. Their native area lies to the west and north-west, including the islands of the Inner and Outer Hebrides, and they are divided from Lowlanders by the Highland Line, an imaginary concept straggling from Argyll in the south-west to Sutherland in the north. They are distinguished from lesser breeds by the Gaelic language.

Estimates in this century are that Gaelic-speakers had dwindled to about 100,000 and were still dwindling, but the decline may be arrested by a recent revival of interest in Gaelic culture, even outside the Highlands. And in this small group there is a wide diversity of accent which marks out a Ross-shire man from a native of Skye or another island.

Gaelic, according to the Gael, was the language spoken in the Garden of Eden, and there is no documentary evidence to disprove the claim. He also believes that Gaelic was the first tongue to create rhyming poetry. The Gael and his culture are not to be dismissed lightly, though Lowlanders sometimes refer to him as a teuchter, an obscure word with connotations of stubbornness and thickness.

The language, imported in one of those migrations, is not a freak. Like virtually all European languages it is a branch of the lost mother-tongue called Proto-Indo-European. Various subdivisions of Celtic survive on the western extremities of Europe—Scotland, Ireland, Wales, the Isle of Man, Cornwall and Brittany.

In modern times, Highlander and Lowlander have intermingled, and there are more people of Highland descent in the city of Glasgow than there are in the Highlands. But if we are to understand the Scots we

7

must remember that Highland and Lowland cultures were and are distinct.

. . . Highland and Lowland cultures were and are distinct

People have noticed that the Scot is both friendly and prickly. It may have something to do with the old Highland clan system.

The clan was a family business. The Frasers clung together, were sometimes friendly with the Mackays and sometimes hostile. The MacGregors clung together and at various times were hostile to almost everybody. There were so many Campbells that some Campbells hated other Campbells. This casual enmity was confused by the Highland reverence for hospitality and good manners. Highlanders may sometimes be devious, dilatory and downright dishonest, but they are polite. The Gaelic language has no dirty words.

8

The Gael in modern history was a crofter and a fisherman, and many Gaels still are. He is both open and clannish. He has his own poetry and his own music, which is beautiful, and recognisable from the extensive use of the pentatonic scale. The traditional entertainment of the Highlands is still the ceilidh, basically an informal concert at which everyone present performs. Strangers will notice that nobody at a ceilidh ever interupts or ignores a performer, or joins in a song unless invited. The kilt is still worn by some Gaels, especially on ceremonial occasions, and the great Highland bagpipe has made its mark on the world from India to Texas. The national sport is shinty, which looks like a form of hockey with no rules. The equivalent of the bully-off takes place with the ball in mid-air. It is driven prodigious distances in one of the fastest sports in the world, and broken limbs are common.

The kilt, and the clan tartan as we know it, are probably modern inventions. Tartan was forbidden by law, under penalty of transportation, after the unsuccessful Scottish rebellion under Bonnie Prince Charlie in 1745. By the time the prohibition was repealed in 1792, the original Highlanders had lost the habit, but it was restored and transformed by an odd quirk of history.

In 1822, when King George IV made his visitation to Edinburgh, Scottish history was wreathed in romance, largely through the novels of Walter Scott, and by a coincidence, there were two brothers Sobieski who were charming polite Edinburgh society and claiming to be descendants of Prince Charlie. They also claimed, though they were cagey about producing the evidence, to have a manuscript entitled *Vestiarium Scoticum* which had been found in a monastery in Cadiz, of all places. This book purported to describe the precise colours and patterns exclusive to each of the old Scottish clans.

The idea is improbable, and Walter Scott himself thought very little of it. It is more likely that the old clansman took pains *not* to be too easily recognisable as a Campbell or a MacGregor. But the times were ripe for romantic notions, the King himself had a kilt made for his massive figure, and fashionable society started to trace its Highland origins and dress accordingly.

Still, if clan tartan is a delusion, it is a harmless and colourful delusion, and the Scottish kilt is quite as rational and comfortable as trousers. The late Oliver Brown, a kindly and gifted firebrand of Scottish nationalism, wore it constantly, and discovered a medical theory that the wearing of trousers could promote infertility in men. There is another theory that the sporran slung in front of the kilt is a phallic, or at least a pubic, symbol.

The kilt helps to demonstrate the contradictory nature of the Scots—schizophrenia would be too heavy a word for it. They have a passion for progress and subversion, and at the same time a reverence for fixed traditions. While other fashions, in men's trousers for instance, constantly change, the kilt remains fixed and immutable, a sartorial museum piece.

With or without the kilt, the Gael has a streak of melancholy which permeates his poetry and music, along with a nostalgia for a lost golden age. It is a product of quite recent history (see John Telfer Dunbar's *Highland Costume*, in this series).

The economy of the Highlands in clan times was at subsistence level, with a bit of crofting, a bit of fishing, a bit of feuding, a bit of cattle rustling. The clan chieftains were sometimes hereditary, but just as commonly elected champions. This all changed dramatically around the time of the Napoleonic Wars, when there was a booming demand for meat, and the Highlands were suddenly seen as ideal sheep ground. There then occurred the monstrous inhumanity remembered still as the Highland Clearances, or as the landlords called them, the Highland Improvements.

It was not merely a matter of bringing sheep in, but of driving human beings out, and they were driven by the lairds whose family duty it was to protect them. There was money in it. A few men can manage thousands of sheep on thousands of acres, and the system does not need or want a large human population. When the simplicity of this got to the lairds, the Clearances were on.

Cottages were burned down to speed up evictions—occasionally with the crofters still inside them—and the clans were scattered. Some were merely evicted, or driven to barren stretches of coast to study starvation; but in other cases clansmen and their families were seized forcibly and dragged to rickety ships to be sent to the colonies like slaves. A society and a way of life were virtually destroyed.

The rest of Britain, almost the rest of Scotland, was hardly aware of this. It was all far away, and like the American Indians, the Highlanders were different, they were Other, aliens with strange customs and a barbarous language.

The Clearances went on for a century. They are now in the past, but the memory is strong, and music and poetry sustain it.

'From the lone shieling of the misty island
   Mountains divide us, and the waste of seas—
Yet still the blood is strong, the heart is Highland,
   And we in dreams behold the Hebrides!'

It is surprising that there is anyone left to croon the old songs, but the Highlanders remaining are stubborn and durable, they still speak their Gaelic and see life in their own way—often a slow and easy way which can irritate incomers. There is an old tale of an Englishman in the Highlands who realised that the pace of life was rather like that of rural Spain, and asked if there was a Gaelic word equivalent to *mañana*.

"There is a similar word," his host told him, "but it does not have the same connotations of urgency."

Visitors are sometimes infected with the condition known as the West Coast Rot, and find that they have no time to do anything because of the number of other things they have no time to do. It can be good for the soul, and it is worth making an effort to know the gentle, tough Highlander and his way of life.

In some places this is becoming harder to find in modern times because of yet another invasion. The charm of the Highlands is so appealing to visitors that in recent decades hundreds of outsiders, from the Lowlands, from England, even from abroad, have bought themselves little cottages in that lonely land. This incursion provides a welcome enough bit of variety in itself, but in some of the northern villages the holiday-home population has almost swamped the original population. Plockton, in Wester Ross, a village of rare beauty, is so popular among visitors that over a third of the houses are now owned by strangers, and when they have spent their few summer weeks enjoying the place, and then left for the south, their houses are shuttered and deserted and a winter death descends on the village. The outside world's pressure on Gaeldom goes on.

(2) The Lowland dichotomy   It is even more difficult to isolate a homogeneous type of Scottish Lowlander, but the visitor may notice that Lowland Scots too speak a variety of strange tongues, and that they are sometimes fierce rather than gentle in matters of religion. To understand both, we have to return to history again.

. . . a brisk two-way trade in cattle-stealing . . .

From the thirteenth century onwards, Scotland maintained a turbulent and confused relationship with its larger neighbour, England. Since communications were poor, the Scots developed in their own ways and largely ignored the land to the south, apart from a brisk two-way trade in cattle-stealing over the Scotland-England border which occasionally broke out into armed brawls. English monarchs, however, sometimes assumed that their kingdom included Scotland, and appointed viceroys and district officers to keep it in order. To settle a squabble among rivals for the Scottish throne, Edward I appointed John Baliol king of the

Scots. Baliol was the celebrated Toom Tabbard (Empty Coat) of Scottish history, regarded by Edward as no more than a lackey. When the lackey showed signs of independence, Edward swept down on Scotland, trounced and dismissed him.

The fight for Scottish self-determination next fell to the unaristocratic William Wallace, who brilliantly organised a war of liberation. He was finally defeated, possibly because the Scottish nobles felt it beneath them to follow a commoner. The struggle was taken up by Robert Bruce, who did win, to become undoubted King of Scots.

The Stewart dynasty which followed Bruce was a mixed collection, and the trouble with England went on and on; and we arrive at a very complicated situation in the sixteenth century, when the English army defeated the Scots at Solway Moss, and King James, fifth of the Stewarts, died in despair. Next in line was the beautiful naïve Mary, reared in France and knowing nothing about Scotland's complex plight.

Henry VIII of England, like his ancestors, was determined to incorporate Scotland into his sovereignty. At the same time, he had quarrelled with the Pope and declared an independent religion for England. The Stewarts, including Mary, were devoted Roman Catholics.

And at the same time, the religious Reformation had reached Scotland, but in its own peculiarly Scottish form and quite unconnected with Henry's. In Scotland, the rejection of Rome was embodied in John Knox, whose Protestantism called for the abolition of bishops and priests and hierarchy and the establishment of every man's equality in the sight of God. It was a hard, spare religion without pomp or frills, and some modern Scots blame it for the sense of guilt that afflicts them, in its rejection of the pleasant comforts of life like dancing and music and fashion and sex. No doubt they exaggerate; but Knox's followers were capable of a pathological hatred of simple joys. One of them (not the master himself) condemned the practice of reading from Scripture at graveside services, 'in case it should excite libidinous thoughts'.

To anyone who has stood by a Scottish grave on a bleak winter's day, the notion of being driven mad with lust by a few verses from Exodus is far-fetched; but a Scot who is really set on hunting down sin will always find some.

We had, then, the rugged fiery John Knox preaching the gospel of simplicity and self-denial, and at the same time the exuberant young queen revering her crucifix and hoping to get some fun out of life. In a way, John Knox won in the end, since he survived to a goodly age (in which he took a teenage bride), Mary was lured to England by her cousin, Henry's daughter Elizabeth, and executed on a trumped-up charge as a possible rival to the English throne; and Scotland became a Protestant country. The old Catholic-Protestant hostility lingered on, all the same, in Scotland.

Romantics of today are drawn, retrospectively, to the charm of Mary, and they see Knox as the grim anti-life-force of Calvinism which they believe has oppressed and soured the Scottish character. Other Scots see Mary as the Scarlet Woman of Rome, the agent of popery, and Knox as the champion of freedom.

Both sides are right and wrong. Mary was all right, and she was not particularly bigoted. She was trapped in a historical situation too fearsome for an unpolitical young woman, and did her pathetic best.

What John Knox did do for the Scottish character was to confirm and revitalise the principle that all men

Other Scots see Mary as the Scarlet Woman of Rome . . .

are equal in the sight of God. In leading the opposition
to Rome he was not merely concerned with doctrine,
but with the deeply Scottish idea that every man is his
own priest and can consult the Deity without making an
appointment. Religious democracy was no small
advance in the world of his time, and the inheritance has
survived. The Scots believe in equality, they believe
that all human beings are Jock Tamson's bairns. They
do have their share of puffed-up poltroons and petty
tyrants and sycophants, but the generality of Scots are
not much impressed by them.

After Elizabeth herself was dead, and Mary's son
James became king of both Scotland and England, there
was an event that affected Scots to their roots, in the

publication of the Bible in English under James's patronage. This was something that the Scottish Protestants had to applaud. Holy Writ was now available to the common man, without the intervention of popes or prelates, in the language of the common man.

But it was not quite the language of the very common man. It was, naturally, an English-English Bible, written in King's English, or Standard English. This was in effect the East Midlands dialect of English, which was adopted as standard for the best of political and administrative reasons: it was spoken by the heaviest concentration of population in the country, which included Parliament and Court.

It was a language capable of magnificence, and in the early seventeenth century it was in magnificent flower, the tongue that Shakespeare spake. Now, it is true that a national language may be created from a hotch-potch of dialects by a single poet, as Dante crystallised Italian, and Pushkin Russian. The influence of Shakespeare on English is not negligible. The King's English of the Authorised Version of the Bible was splendid, even if it was merely a language form chosen for administrative convenience. It was very different from Scots-English.

The development of the Scottish tongue has been mentioned earlier (see David Murison's *The Guid Scots Tongue*, in this series). It was, by this time, very much itself, and the centuries of enmity with England had intensified its distinctness. During these centuries the Scots were in a loose alliance with France against the Auld Enemy, there was some kind of trade with France which had its own minor influences on the Scots' vocabulary. At the same time Scotland had trade and intercourse with the northern Germanic-language countries, and this influenced Scots-language usages and pronunciations, like kirk for church and hoose for house; or in some cases the Norse contact probably simply helped to consolidate Old English usages which were being changed and modified in England itself.

The differences between Scots-English and English-English are not just a question of accent. To offer a simple example: When a cockney says "Dahn ve ill", he thinks he is saying "Down the hill"—and indeed he is, as long as his listener agrees. However, when a Scotsman says "Doon the brae", he does *not* imagine he is saying "Down the hill". He knows he is saying "Doon the brae". He could say "Down the hill" if he chose. When he refers to an oxter, he is not trying and failing to pronounce 'armpit'. Oxter is a different word, from an equally respectable source.

Nevertheless, the arrival of the English Bible was a trauma for the Scots. Being intensely religious and disputatious, they clasped the translation to their bosoms and discovered something shameful: that while in their everyday lives they spoke of everyday things in Scots, God spoke in English. The nation has not entirely recovered from this delusion. Down to this day there are Scots who feel that their language is not quite proper, that ideally they should speak 'normal' English like real English speakers. They feel, in a word, that their native language is *déclassé*. And there are geographical or sociological pockets in Scotland in which people do their best to deny their linguistic roots and talk like well-bred southerners. The noises they make, known variously as Morningside, Kelvinside and pan-loaf, are hilarious, as always when people try to ape their betters (and I use the word 'betters' with due thought—a real Englishman must be better than an imitation Englishman).

Thus the Scottish character is split down the middle. The division is deepened by the fact that when King

James chose to make his home in London—he knew where the fleshpots were—his courtiers and hangers-on were close behind him. The Scottish gentry made certain their children were educated in England, to have the stain of provincialism rubbed away. In a company of Scotsmen you can always identify the aristocrat by his English accent.

RELIGIOUS HEAT The dichotomy in religion lingered on, sometimes lethally. Catholic and Presbyterian in turn persecuted each other until the bloody business was finished when King William of Orange defeated the Catholic King James II and ascended the throne in 1689. For the study of one kind of Scottish Lowlander, we may leap from there to modern times.

William of Orange was believed by many modern Scots to have been the champion of Protestantism against popery, but was not. He was almost without religious animus, made gifts to convents, and would have no nonsense from Scottish Presbyterians who wanted to impose their faith by law and force on other people. But the legend will not be laid. William, King Billy, remains the hero of the more fervent Scot in the western Lowlands for what they believe was his blow against the papacy at the Battle of the Boyne.

Therefore, one of the enthusiasms of, for instance, the city of Glasgow today is religious heat. It is a minority sport, but the minority is energetic. Many thousands of Scots in Glasgow and elsewhere draw power and fire from the conviction that Rome still plots to take them over; but, in the words of their slogan, No Surrender.

This enthusiasm was fed by immigration from Ireland in modern times, notably during the Hungry

Forties of the last century when blight struck the Irish potato crop, and the Irish population was reduced eventually, in death and flight, by three-quarters. Many, then and in later waves, came to the west of Scotland, where their odd customs, their alien religion and their incomprehensible speech made them strange and dangerous animals. When the Fenian movement of Irish rebellion became troublesome to the British Government, all immigrant Irish Catholics were taken to be Fenians, doubtless plotting to murder innocent Protestants in their beds.

Historically illiterate Scots have not lost this suspicion, and it is interesting that they still draw inspiration from Ireland itself—Northern Ireland, that is, the home of the Orange movement. On or around the Boyne anniversary, 12th July ('Twelfth of July, the Papes will die'), they organise the Orange Walk, with marvellously colourful banners and music of the flute, the pipes and the piano-accordion. These parades are impressive and sometimes alarming, and from a safe distance make an interesting tourist spectacle.

There is also bigotry and suspicion among some Scottish Roman Catholics. No doubt the hostility has unrecognised economic undertones. The original Irish immigrants, poverty-stricken and uneducated, were a source of cheap labour which endangered the employment of the natives. An interesting development of this is that if you move through Glasgow today you will find a disproportionate number of public houses and betting shops bearing Irish names. Excluded from higher education and the learned professions by their poverty and illiteracy, the Irish found that drink and gambling were almost the only industries in which they could rise in the world. The social and educational gap between the Catholics and the rest of the population has noticeably closed, and in law and politics and elsewhere the descendants of immigrants have found notable success. But a Catholic schoolmaster insisted to me recently that the Scottish Catholics were still a backward group.

GLASGOW—TRAINED IN SURVIVAL Anyone who enjoys a discussion on religion is wise to walk carefully in the Glasgow area; and nowhere more carefully than at Parkhead and Ibrox Park, the homes of Scotland's two greatest football teams, Celtic (Catholic) and Rangers (Protestant). I mention the teams in alphabetical order to avoid bias, but there is no way of avoiding an accusation of bias in this context.

. . . Scotland's two greatest football teams . . .

21

Rangers and Celtic, in spite of the occasional emergence of other football clubs such as Aberdeen or Heart of Midlothian, are the supremes of Scottish football, and they draw their support not only from their neighbourhoods but from all over Lowland Scotland. They are very good. Their supporters are loyal, and a visible proportion on both sides is violent. Glasgow is, in fact, a violent city, but a stranger should not be deterred by that generalisation. Although it is my native city and I am therefore prejudiced, I must still say that it is one of the friendliest cities anywhere, and on the whole, its people are kindly, tough, witty and welcoming. It is possible to go for years in the city without seeing or meeting violence, especially if one stays away from Rangers-Celtic football matches. And it may be (I suggest this with diffidence and even doubt) that the occasional eruptions of violence merely represent natural exuberance gone to excess.

The character of the typical Glaswegian has been tempered by a history of fairly continuous hardship, recession and depression. The city has always had an enormous mercantile and industrial energy, with linen, tobacco, shipbuilding and heavy engineering, but most of the trades and industries it embraced turned out to be in the process of decay at the time. The effect, historically, is one of gloom, but the people who survived these vicissitudes emerge as people trained in survival with good humour. They are even sometimes suspicious of good times—perhaps a relic from John Knox—and suspect that luck will probably have to be paid for later.

Stoic pessimism, at its Glaswegian best, becomes joyous fatalism.

On the one hand, we have the football hostility, though even this makes its contribution to the uncrushable humour of the Scots, as in the story of a stranger who entered an exclusively Rangers pub, leading a live alligator, and asked, "Do you serve Catholics in here?" The barman, eyeing the pet, hurriedly said yes. "Right," said the customer. "A pint for me and a Catholic for my pal."

On the other hand is Partick Thistle football club, whose fans tell jokes against their team or themselves. A man telephoned the ground one Saturday and asked when the game was due to start. "What time would suit you, sir?" the manager asked. And there was an occasion when the Supporters' Club had assembled to travel to an away game, but had to give it up because the tandem had broken down.

EDINBURGH BREEDING   There is, among Glaswegians, a dislike of Edinburgh, which luckily is largely for joke purposes. A club exists, composed of men of both cities, whose object is solemnly to maintain and increase the enmity between the two. Edinburghers claim that the finest thing that ever came out of Glasgow was the train service to Edinburgh. A Glasgow club held a prize draw in which the first prize was a week in Edinburgh, and the second prize was two weeks in Edinburgh.

Edinburgh regards Glasgow as coarse, Glasgow dismisses Edinburgh as cold. In the version of Jack House, a Glasgow journalist, people in Edinburgh equate breeding with good form, while Glaswegians accept it as good fun. Edinburgh hospitality, according to a Glaswegian, is a man in the Capital City opening his door to a visitor and saying, "Come in, come in—you'll have had your tea."

Edinburgh, at least at its heart, is a noble city, and it

is difficult to emerge into Princes Street without a lifting of the heart. Glasgow has nothing to equal a main street with a castle rock and a genuine castle on one side, and a view of a genuine rustic hill, Arthur's Seat, as an alternative pleasure. It has succeeded in keeping the *bourgeois* grace of its New Town undemolished, even if the fine terraces have lost many of their families and acquired office tenants instead. The High Street, the Grassmarket, the Royal Mile, still reek with history. And the natives are not all that savage.

Edinburgh is accustomed to visitors in the mass . . .

Edinburgh is accustomed to visitors in the mass, during the Edinburgh Festival and at other times, and it absorbs them without fuss. It may be true that Capital people seem less warm and forthcoming than the couthy

Glaswegians. They even use less coarse language. But in my own experience this is a superficial quibble. The social life, in the pubs and the good supply of eating-houses, is lively and genial, and the personal warmth is near the surface.

The city has its own history, of course, a history only lightly touched by industrial revolutions and collapses. It is the home of Government and the Law, and it can take a douce pride in the notable characters who wrote its history with their lives—Darnley, husband of Mary, Queen of Scots, who with a party of drunken friends murdered his wife's innocent secretary Rizzio out of bad temper; Deacon Brodie, pillar of society by day and master criminal by night, and the inspiration of R. L. Stevenson's Jekyll and Hyde; Walter Scott, who did no harm whatever and brought lustre to his native country; Burke and Hare, sometimes thought to have been grave-robbers but who were in fact commercial murderers providing material for anatomists.

Yes, in strolling through Edinburgh a man can feel the throb of history through his boot-soles. But the native Edinburgher, sometimes laconic, carries the burden of history lightly, takes only a mild pride in his innate superiority, and is a very nice chap.

A HARD PLACE, ABERDEEN   That is the legend, at least. It is, certainly, made of granite, and it stays clean and hard and glittering, the Silver City with the Golden Sands. It is hard, because it was surrounded with cold hard farming land and flanked by the cold grey sea and the grim business of fishing. Its language bears little relation to the Glasgow twang because Aberdeen is a very self-contained town and some of its people still regard people fifty miles away as foreigners. During

25

much of its life it had more traffic with Norway than with the south of Scotland—they say the composer Grieg was the grandson of an Aberdeenshire farmer called Greig, who in turn was possibly descended from an incoming Norwegian, but I cannot swear to that.

The Aberdonians are Lowlanders, not Highlanders, though the city is so far to the north. There is no Gaelic tradition here. The common greeting between friends is "Fit like?" ("What like?"), which demonstrates both warmth and economy of breath. This is the home of the Aberdeen joke, in which at least twenty people get out of every taxi, moths fly out when a purse is opened, and one citizen even had a trained moth in his purse to chew the date off his railway ticket. The Aberdonians themselves produce these jokes, and there may be something in them, in a city that has had to drag a living from hard earth and chill water.

'The people who purposive and with strategy,' George Bruce described his compatriots, 'established a northern city. . . .' Yes, there is a sense of purpose and strategy. The Aberdonian is nobody's fool, knows how many beans make five, and so on. He also lives in a city a good deal colder than even Edinburgh. A southern friend of mine who went to university there spent two months of baffled misery before he realised that he needed long woollen underwear before he could feel normal. Glaswegians complain that Aberdeen is too much like a village, and that it is impossible to nod to a person of the other sex at one end of Union Street without having it reported instantly at the other end, usually to her mother. Some people find this village feeling cosy rather than repellent. Aberdeen is quite a together place.

The city, and its citizens, are today at the centre of the North Sea oil business, and doubtless are making good business from it. But the changes are less obvious than might be expected and the character of the natives seems as durable and unaltered as before.

This grey, or silver, city has its own traditions of hospitality, even apart from the well-organised tourist trade; though it does take some time to crack the surface. But I myself have cracked it regularly, and found the cold northern city warm enough for a Glaswegian.

. . . AND THE PEOPLE OF DUNDEE The Dundonian is difficult to nail down. Like Glasgow, Dundee has endured cycles of prosperity and penury, and in recent times has succeeded physically in tearing out its own heart and exiling many of its people to bleak suburbs which daunt the spirit. There is an identity problem in the Dundonian, I think. The one stable and enduring industry of the area is the publishing house of D. C. Thomson, which publishes the folksy *Sunday Post* and the *Weekly News*, and a string of women's and boys' papers, and it has been suggested by a native that the citizens have lost touch with reality and imagine they are living in a *Sunday Post* comic strip.

Their most potent literary tradition, apart from the continuing mastery of the D. C. Thomson press, is William Topaz McGonagall, Edinburgh-born of Irish parents and the most celebrated bad poet of the English language.

'Beautiful Railway Bridge of the Silvery Tay!
With your numerous arches and pillars in so grand
    array,
And your central girders, which seem to the eye
To be almost towering to the sky.
The greatest wonder of the day,

And a great beautification to the River Tay,
Most beautiful to be seen,
Near by Dundee and the Magdalen Green.'

That is a fair sample of McGonagall's work. But McGonagall, the incomer, may provide a clue to the character of his adopted city; because the beautiful railway bridge whose praises he sang soon collapsed, in 1879, with the death of ninety passengers travelling north for the New Year holiday, and McGonagall, without the least dismay, at once jumped in to create a fresh poetic gem on the Tay Bridge Disaster. And when the ruin was rebuilt, he was standing at the ready to indite an epic address to the beautiful *new* railway bridge of the Silvery Tay.

It isn't so much the opportunism that characterises the Dundonian as the rueful acceptance of triumph and disaster as events beyond human control and things to be accepted.

So the Dundonian grumbles a good deal, and with good reason, but he dreams too. The beautiful new railway bridge of the Silvery Tay is quite nice, by the way, and so is the new road bridge of the Silvery Tay which rather overshadows the old bridge nowadays.

THE FAIR CITY Perth, the other Scottish town which claims to be a city, was once briefly the capital, and lies more or less in the centre of the country; it arouses all my own ambivalence, and I am not alone. Physically, it is one of the urban delights of Scotland, with tiny old tenements on its main streets jostling with department stores, and the elegant mansions along the Inches (islands), the higher reaches of the Tay bustling beside it, and the lush rolling farmland of Perthshire cuddling it all round.

Its own fine, neglected and short-lived poet William Soutar used to look at those mansions, which showed the observer no sign of life, but where, inside, the professional classes were 'thrang and thriving'. Other people have gained the same impression. A charming, settled, oddly in-turned place, careless of progress, mildly agreeable to strangers but incurious and engrossed in its own private affairs.

If this seems dismissive, I can only plead that there has to be some aspect of the Scottish character to which I can give a poor review.

THE CHAMPION OF THE COMMON There would be no point in trying to analyse Scotland's 'landward areas'—the county districts outside the big towns. Ayrshire is worth mentioning for a hundred reasons, but I include it simply because of Robert Burns, who was born in Alloway in 1759 and died thirty-seven years later in Dumfriesshire.

And Robert Burns must be included in any survey of the Scots because he is at once the archetypal and the fantasy Scot. Much may be deduced about the contradictory nature of the Scots by a look at the National Bard, his work and his life. In a great degree, Burns both discovered and created the Scot's sense of identity. No matter whether he was a great poet, or merely a good one, he struck a chord that is still ringing in Scotsmen's minds after two centuries—and in fact ringing in the minds of Russians, Japanese, Americans and other people even stranger.

Burns was born and grew up in poverty, the son of a dogged but unsuccessful tenant farmer. He was gifted with manic energy and shadowed by undiagnosed rheumatic fever contracted in boyhood, which killed him at the end. He had a fair education, for his time, and in an age when the Scottish nation was a poor thing, without even a Parliament of its own, and people of taste and ambition revered everything that was fine, and English, Burns started pouring out, in fair torrents, his verses in the broad Ayrshire tongue of his surroundings. He was not the first. There were good models in Henryson and Fergusson. Still, writing in Scots was not the obvious road to public acclaim. He did not give a damn.

He had read English poets (he was a particular admirer of Pope); but he was unshakeably himself. Regardless of history, or because of history, he was glad to be a Scot, to be natural, to see clearly and feel deeply and speak openly. He was endlessly up against the small-time established authority of the day—the pious, the hypocritical, the narrow clergy—and in love with mundane things—the earth, nature, friendship, drink, girls. He was impelled to strike out for the freedom of the natural man, and let the chips fall where they might. He chose to be common, and became the champion of the common. If there is one clarion-call with which every Scotsman will agree (at least formally) it is 'A man's a man for a' that'.

His dismissal of religious cant is still alive and vibrating, because religious cant is still alive in Scotland. There is an old but contemporary joke (and by a people's jokes shall ye know them) about a young minister who was elected to a charge in the Highlands, and met an elderly parishioner on a country road one Sunday afternoon.

"You'll be on an errand of mercy, Minister," said the elder.

"No, I am merely taking a stroll to enjoy the fresh air."

"Oh, we don't hold with a man taking pleasure on the Sabbath, Minister."

"Come come, our own Lord didn't hesitate to pluck an ear of corn on the Sabbath."

"No, and in this parish we never thought any the better of him for it."

At our most religious, and our most silly, we are capable of anything. But we are also capable of juggling repression and indulgence so that we can enjoy both with a straight face. The old Kirk of Burns's Day, in its lunatic fringes, managed the trick through the Doctrine of Election, which brings comfort to those who embrace it and damnation to everybody else. The Doctrine, which is marvellously perverted Judaism, teaches that each human being is born into the world either as one of God's Elect, saved from conception and guaranteed entry to heaven, or doomed from the start through sins committed by his or her ancestors; that the Elect may break every law and receive forgiveness, while the damned can emulate the saints and still have a very nasty end throughout eternity.

Burns encapsulated this doctrine, and virtually swept it into contemptuous oblivion, in his poem 'Holy Willie's Prayer'. Holy Willie is one of the Elect—it is interesting that believers assumed that they themselves were elected, and the damned were Other People. Let me quote a few verses, in the hope that they may send readers to seek out the full text.

'O Thou that in the heavens does dwell!
Wha, as it pleases best Thysel,
Sends ane to heaven and ten to h—ll,
    A' for Thy glory;
And no for ony guid or ill
    They've done before Thee!

I bless and praise Thy matchless might,
When thousands Thou hast left in night,
That I am here before Thy sight,
    For gifts and grace
A burning and a shining light,
    To a' this place.
. . . .

When frae my mither's womb I fell,
Thou might hae plungèd me in hell,
To gnash my gums, to weep and wail,
    In burnin lakes,
Where damnèd devils roar and yell,
    Chain'd to their stakes.

Holy Willie

Yet I am here, a chosen sample,
To show Thy grace is great and ample;
I'm here, a pillar o' Thy temple,
    Strong as a rock;
A guide, a ruler, and example
    To a' Thy flock.
. . . .

O L—d—yestreen—Thou kens—wi Meg—
Thy pardon I sincerely beg:
O, may't ne'er be a livin plague,
    To my dishonor!
And I'll ne'er lift a lawless leg
    Again upon her!
. . . .

Maybe Thou lets this fleshly thorn
Buffet Thy servant e'en and morn
Lest he owre proud and high should turn
    That he's sae gifted:
If sae, Thy hand maun e'en be borne
    Until Thou lift it.
. . . .

L—d, mind Gaun Hamilton's deserts;
He drinks, and swears, and plays at cartes,
Yet has sae mony takin arts
    Wi Great and Sma',
Frae G—d's ain Priest the people's hearts
    He steals awa.
. . . .

And when we chasten'd him therefore
Thou kens how he bred sic a splore,
And set the warld in a roar
    O' laughin at us:
Curse Thou his basket and his store
    Kail and potatoes.

. . . .
> But L—d remember me and mine
> Wi' mercies temporal and divine;
> That I for grace and gear may shine
>   Excell'd by nane!
> And a' the glory shall be Thine,
>   AMEN! AMEN!'

If he had done nothing else, Burns would be worth remembering for Holy Willie. He did much else. He did not merely love the lassies, he did something about it. In this, he lived out the fantasies of decent men who fain would, but dare not. He defied. He maintained. Even his weaknesses take on a quality of universality. When he went to Edinburgh and was lionised by polite society, had a rather prissy affair with the trivial Mrs Maclehose and took her advice to write in proper English (poor stuff it was, too), we hardly blame him because most of us have been dazzled by an unattainable beauty, and most of us have a touch of the snob in us.

Over the piece, he was a man; a man's man and a woman's man. He was ourselves, but risen to heroic and tragic stature. And he was Scotland. As much as Wallace or Bruce, he handed back to the Scots their sense of entity. If you would understand the Scots you must understand that even among the mim-mouthed, the mean, the craven, the money-counters, Burns is the man we would like to be, and sometimes feel we are. Brave, tender, dashing and kindly. And irresistible to women.

THE UNEQUAL SCOTS The Holy Willie is still with us. But it would be wrong to claim a Scottish monopoly of Holy Willies. Highly placed people in such

34

un-Scottish places as China, Haiti, the United States and Uganda have displayed the conviction that virtue is for other people and that they themselves are entitled to use any dirty trick available for their own aggrandisement. The psychopath is not a Scottish invention (though, as we shall see, there are Scots who might claim it was, since they believe the Scots invented everything).

Maybe this brand of psychopath emerges in a peculiarly Scottish form, however. Here is a small country with a literate and articulate population which could nevertheless support and tolerate a class of loonies who were patently loonies but who could still demand respect and attention. This is the sad song of all mankind. But in Scotland it is compounded by the national reverence for equality, which is not a universal preoccupation. The Scots succeeded in distorting egalitarianism.

If every man is equal to every other man, after all, then there is something offensive about one man who presumes to be better than another man—better at arithmetic, or reading, or knowing more about the stars. Egalitarianism gone berserk means that nobody should be noticeably superior to anybody, and in politics and administration in Scotland this means the assumption of power by dedicated nonentities whose claim to authority is that they are just as ignorant as the next man. In Scottish public life, mediocrity has always been a useful qualification, and the notable exceptions only make the fact more obvious. In Scottish politics, in any age, a man of moderate intellect has stood out like Everest, though in better company he might be no higher than a telegraph pole.

Why? The natural indolence of the Scot, perhaps, who would rather talk about politics than get mixed up in them, and who leaves the quirky business of involvement to men of action and natural leaders. Let us define a natural leader: he is a man who is afraid to go anywhere by himself.

This section is about the unequal Scots who have insisted on emerging regardless.

We have James Watt. I was taught as a schoolchild that Watt held a spoon to the spout of a steaming kettle and discovered that the jet pushed the spoon away, revealing to the boy the power that was to transform the world. This is not *entirely* true. I have repeated the experiment, and it does not work. The available power contained in steam emerging from a kettle is almost nil, and will certainly not move a spoon. It is also a fact that steam engines were puffing away before Watt arrived. The creditable fact is that Watt took the primitive designs of his day and developed them into an efficient commercial engine which did transform the world. But as Scots, we have a compulsion to claim miracles when an intelligent conjuring trick is quite sufficient.

Watt soon left for England, where there were opportunities for him to thrive and prosper on his engineering talent. Once he was safely away, with his superior intelligence and energy, the Scots could safely be proud of him, and take credit for his work.

William Murdoch was an Ayrshire lad of parts who invented gas lighting. It took courage and stubbornness as well as inspiration, because his patrons were convinced that the gas running through the pipes to the outlet was on fire all the way along, and would incinerate cities. But Murdoch was stubborn enough for the task, to the point of eccentricity. For instance, he had fashioned for himself, on a lathe, a bowler-hat made from a solid block of wood, and he wore this on his journey to the English Midlands, where people were more receptive to his crazy ideas than the Scots would have been.

Long before, William Paterson had discovered in himself a financial genius. As a good and shrewd Scot, he deployed it in inventing the Bank of England. His compatriot John Law, a regrettably impulsive individual who killed a man in a duel, left Scotland for his own reasons, and master-minded the transformation of State finance for Louis XVI of France.

Alexander Graham Bell did invent the telephone. He did it in America, where it is still synonymous with his name.

To be fair, not every unusual Scot was compelled to emigrate for his own good. And for a country of a few million souls the list of Scottish innovators is imposing. Napier gave the world the logarithm, Lord Kelvin made significant contributions to electricity, Simpson pioneered anaesthetics, Fleming found penicillin (in England) and Watson-Watt devised radar.

Being touchy, and still having that small-nation complex which compels us to bluster, we believe that a Scotsman, Henry Bell, invented the steamship. Henry Bell invented nothing. He was a shrewd businessman who saw a connection between boats and power, and he ordered a hull from a builder and a steam engine from another chap to be fitted in it. It wasn't even the first thing of its kind, since Robert Fulton already had a steamship plying commercially in America. However, these facts should not be put too forcibly to the average Scotsman for fear of shattering his view of the universe.

For that matter, although our native son Logie Baird did develop (in London) a workable form of television, the groundwork had already been laid in a scanning disc devised by a meddlesome Russian, Nipkov; and the Baird process turned out to be a dead end, because it relied on mechanical scanning, a clumsy, primitive process which had no hope against the electronic system. All the same, let us be fair, this doesn't diminish the stature of Baird as an innovator or reduce him as a man of vision. I am merely indicating the Scots' passion for claiming to be first in everything.

There are, in fact, even wilder claims which I myself would support from perverseness. The Scotsman MacOwski composed the *Pathétique*, MacYavelli invented diplomacy, and MacRoni wireless telegraphy. If you believe everything a Scotsman tells you about Scotsmen, you are believing anything.

ONLY A GAME Golf is another matter. Lesser breeds make impertinent claims in this field (as they do with the bagpipe). Historically, an activity resembling golf was found in such an unlikely place as Holland. But the game as we know it grew up in Scotland, and the world's first golf club (in the sense of an association of golfers) was created in Edinburgh. They were, and are, Gentlemen. But egalitarian Scotland is one of the few nations in which golf is for everybody.

There is perhaps something Knoxian about golf, in the sense that a man is struggling symbolically, not with a human opponent, but with his own shortcomings; and that no matter how hard he tries, the destiny of his soul, or his ball, is in the hands of a Greater Power Who works in mysterious ways and against Whose judgement there is no appeal. The Doctrine of Election may even come into it if one considers how often some people can commit every sin in the game and still break par.

But whether golf is a cosmic ritual or only a game, it is a sizeable gift for a small nation to have given to the entire uncivilised world. It is both private and religious, because the most incorrigible two-handicap cheat, discounting the twelve slashes he made in the rough as attempts to kill a snake, knows in his soul that the Great Handicapper was with him, and that his sins are recorded.

It is interesting that few Scottish players today reach the international heights of the competitive game, and this says something about the Scots. Throughout their history they have said: This is the discovery, this is the revelation, this is the path to glory; and then stood aside to see other, lesser people gallop along the path ahead of them. It is all a part of the Scottish conviction that what will be, will be, that we must dree our weird, accept the will of God, and bow our heads to muffle our curses as an American holes out in one.

And it is not only the game that the Scots have donated to the world. With it goes an immense subculture, including the golfing joke. Any observer with the wit to see beyond mechanical, economic or even religious theories about the human condition knows well that the joke is mankind's survival kit, that a good story is more enduring than systems or empires; and that a nation which has opened the floodgates to an ocean of jokes is a nation to be accounted great. I shall not quote any golf jokes. Life and this book are too short.

BLURRING THE EDGES   Whisky is even funnier. In giving whisky to the world, it may be that the Scots have surpassed their donations of engineering, mathematics, theology and neurosis. The Scot in conjunction with whisky must be approached with some respect, and even apprehension, for he regards the national drink with reverence amounting to fatuity.

Just as there is wine snobbery, so there is whisky snobbery, and Scots who have drunk too deep at this well of illusion can make fantastical claims. The most obsessional among them will boast of distinguishing a whisky's parentage, its location and the name of the burn from which the original water was drawn. The best response to such pretences is a respectful nod and a quiet guffaw up the sleeve.

Scotch whisky, fundamentally, is fermented barley made into a kind of beer and then distilled. Its prime attraction is that unlike vodka, for instance, it is rich in impurities. It is a richly adulterated liquor incorporating a wide range of aldehydes, fusel-oils and other magic ingredients, and therefore tastes like whisky rather than denatured nitrogen.

Individual whiskies do vary widely, and their nature is indeed affected by the original source of water, which may be enriched with various intensities of peat and other alluvial matter. Single (unblended) malt whiskies are particularly distinctive, and each one varies from one distilling run to the next, because when the stuff trickles from the still, it retains a lot of these interesting adulterants. The liquor at the beginning of the run is fairly dreadful, likewise the stuff at the tail-end. The glorious nectar comes in the middle, and a man, without computers or slide-rules, has the job of deciding when to stop discarding the early liquid, choose the middle and then switch off the disagreeable dregs. The discarded liquor, naturally, goes back in to be distilled again.

Other whiskies, most whiskies, are made purely for blending with other whiskies, and the ancient craft has been overtaken by the American Coffey still, which creates the potent liquid continuously and invisibly. This would seem to take the mystery out of Scotch, but even with mechanisation, an individual product keeps its individuality and its quiddity, and the job of marrying a dozen or more whiskies into a recognisable recipe is still a quirky thing. A consumer who is not dead to all sense of decency will have no difficulty in telling a blended Haig from a single-malt Islay Mist.

But if he keeps repeating the experiment, actually drinking the stuff each time, he can tell almost nothing, because his taste-buds are quickly washed to sleep. I have seen public demonstrations of whisky-tasting (in fact, I had the good luck to be involved in some) in which proud Scottish aficionados got it all wrong after the first couple of drams. For the hard-liquor enthusiast, Scotch whisky is a noble potation of great variety, and no doubt its distinction does derive something from the air, the hills, the streams and the ancient art of the Scottish distiller. But the sensible man enjoys it without too much histrionic analysis.

Patriotic Scots, or snobs, insist that it must be drunk neat, or at worst diluted with pure Scottish water. Others, who just want a drink, take it any way they please, with ginger ale, soda, lemonade, green-ginger wine, coffee, even vermouth. This last may not be the best way of drinking whisky, but it's a hell of a good way to drink vermouth.

The Scot, and particularly the industrial Scot of the Glasgow area, sometimes chases it with beer. It may seem eccentric to want to chase whisky, but the beer is really there to help to pass the time between drinks. The ritual is to swallow the dram of whisky neat, in one, refrain from choking, grip the top of the skull to prevent explosion, and briskly ingest a gulp of beer to quench the blaze. Drunkenness is quickly produced in this way, but it must regrettably be confessed that the basic Scot takes alcohol for that purpose. Not for him the leisurely swirling, the holding to the light, the sniffing of the bouquet and the epicurean sip. Life is hard in Scotland, and Scotland produced Scotch to blur the jagged edges with the minimum delay.

Many Scots are dedicated non-drinkers.

A PAGAN FESTIVAL Most Scottish folk-rituals tend to involve whisky, but the closest association is between whisky and Hogmanay, known to other English-speaking peoples as New Year's Eve.

New Year is another Scottish tradition which has been eagerly embraced by other peoples in modern times, and they are of course entitled to make what they can of it. In Scotland, it is something highly particular, buried deep in the folk-memory of the people. Hogmanay is a pagan festival, and in modern times it has merely been confused by the determination of the Church to join in and give it a Christian gloss. The Church is entitled to do its best, of course. Its own adjacent rite of Christmas is also an odd compound of old pagan feasts and the New Testament. In fact, the two festivals may well have been the same festival at one time, split into two because earlier Christians felt it right to have a separate day to celebrate the birth of Christ, but couldn't manage to move too far away from the old midwinter rituals.

Whatever the case, the Scottish Hogmanay clings to elements purely humanist and pagan; and since it has been so widely imitated, it may as well be imitated accurately, as it is practised in its country of origin—at least, as it is practised in areas which have escaped being destroyed by urban planning.

It is not just an excuse for a drunken orgy, though there is nothing wrong with that. It *is* a time, admittedly, when abstemious people can have a bucket and feel virtuous. In fact, as a cynical barmaid once remarked to me early in January when the place was full of people boasting about their hangovers, "Hogmanay is strictly for amateurs."

. . . when abstemious people can have a bucket and feel virtuous

But enough of this flippancy. Hogmanay is a time to purify, a time to hope, a time to discard old feuds and a time to keep friendships in repair. Hogmanay (the origin of the word remains obscure and controversial) is spent in house-cleaning and paying debts, so that no dirt or obligation shall be carried over to besmirch the coming year. In households with coal fires, even the ashes from the fire are removed and carried out of the house a few minutes before midnight.

The day is also a day of sobriety. It is true that this rule is often broken in modern times, simply because both the habit and the stuff are there. We should remember that during most of Scotland's modern history, respectable people drank very little. Alcohol was the curse of the working classes, especially the scruffy working classes, and the indulgence of the rich. The mass of people in the middle, with appearances to keep up and no money to spare, might not touch a drop from one year's end to another. For them, then, the broaching of the bottle at New Year was significant. Nowadays, nearly everybody is at it, and the significance has diminished.

No matter. Traditionally, the household abjures the Stuff, and as the old year creaks to an end, a quiet excitement grows. Then, in an instant, the bells have rung, time past is forgotten gratefully, and the ritual toast is poured. For dour Scots, and even normal Scots, this moment is genuinely pregnant. We do believe (because hope dismisses experience) that this year, this New Year, will be brand new, full of realised dreams and prosperity, that like dead Balder we will be born anew, taller and richer and kinder and more beautiful.

The next significant incident is the arrival of the First Foot, even if this does not happen for hours, or days. The first visitor to the household in the New Year must be male, and dark-haired. He must bring gifts of food and drink, to guarantee the prosperity of the house, and he must be given food and drink in exchange, to placate the dark gods of fate. In other words, he must be given a good time. That is the point of it all. But it must be done in proper style according to the proper rules.

These customs vary from place to place in Scotland, but no matter where, they are taken seriously. The Scot, like other people of Northern Europe, knows that at this bottom end of winter, the world has ritually died and that its rebirth requires due and solemn observances as well as, or including, a good booze-up. In some parts of Ireland, it is the duty of the head of the household at the stroke of midnight to hurl a loaf of bread at the inside of the front door, which is probably all right as long as nobody happens to be coming in at the time.

In England, on the other hand, some apprentice pagans who like the idea of New Year are under the delusion that a First Foot is required merely to arrive with a lump of coal in his hand. This is ignorance. No household objects to a lump of coal, certainly, but it is a ludicrous substitute for the true cargo of the First Foot, that offering of food and drink. The drink should be whisky, though a fine Napoleon brandy would not be spurned; and the food may be anything, but probably includes shortbread or black bun or Dundee cake. It is hard to distinguish black bun from Dundee cake. Both are immensely rich, and an ounce of each weighs an English hundredweight.

The First Foot gives a drink to the company and accepts a drink, and the ritual is complete for the moment. Thereafter, any visitor is welcome, including blonde females. Having played his role, the First Foot is free and unimportant, and may leave to do his thing for other households. And members of the household may have obligations elsewhere as First Foots. Dark-haired men can go missing for days at New Year.

In recent times, Hogmanay was a favoured date for weddings, probably because it was one of the few holiday times in which to incorporate a honeymoon. It is no longer so, but times may get harder and old customs return.

THE TRAVELLING SCOT The Scot is a passionate traveller. With the sea at his doorstep and tough times at his back, it isn't surprising. Especially in the west, it would be hard to find a family without at least one cousin or uncle in Australia or New Zealand or Canada or America. There is a powerful affinity with America, in fact. The late Moray McLaren, an Edinburgher, once accused a Glasgow writer of not noticing that Glasgow was an intensely America-oriented city, and he was right.

The Scots, however, have explored and wandered, but they have never colonised, even when they might have scooped up prizes like the Isle of Man and Rockall. David Livingstone and Mungo Park opened up the African continent for other people to exploit, but Scots have refrained from planting the flag in other lands, except perhaps at Rotary tables. They are expert at assimilation. The archetypal Glaswegian, having decided to shake the dust from his shoes and find a place in the United States, begins to talk like John Wayne on the bus to the airport.

One of the great Scotch comics, Tommy Morgan, described such a traveller, disgusted with his native land, with the poverty and the griminess and the lack of opportunity, finally escaping and landing at Kennedy Airport. And as he was leaving the plane to step on to American soil, he sat on his overnight bag, burst into tears and started signing 'Granny's Hielan' Hame'.

Many people have noticed that a Scotsman's Scottishness increases with his distance from Scotland. They do fit into other communities, but at the drop of a

A Scotsman's Scottishness increases with his distance from Scotland

hat they inaugurate Burns Clubs and Caledonian Societies, and learn Highland dances that would have embarrassed them to death back home in Govan or Craigmillar. At the safe distance of 5,000 miles they even buy kilts and deliberately wear them, at least once a year. The Scot can be a mawkish individual, even when sober.

It shows in our popular music, which alters not with the years. A bright lad can always make a little money by writing a song, preferably in three-four time, about the dear land he has left behind him. In the rest of the Western world, popular music is in a constant ferment. Victorian ballads don't have much in common with the twentieth-century works of Irving Berlin or Johnny

Mercer. These in turn are distinctly dated beside the songs of the Beatles, and the Beatles' style is being nudged aside by new sounds. But the Scottish audience for Scottish songs likes things the way they were, are, and always will be. Jimmy Copeland won a national song competition recently with a comfortable waltz-time ditty proclaiming:

'For these are my mountains
And this is my glen,
The braes of my childhood
Will know me again. . . .'

Nice song. It would have gone down equally well in 1910, because it goes back to the Highland Clearances, and Scottish audiences have an unquenchable lust for nostalgia, as well as a long, confused memory. You could almost organise a marathon concert of nothing but songs yearning for a lost homeland. 'How I wish that I could see my Granny's Hielan' hame'. 'O for one sight of Bonny Loch Leven'. 'There's a wee hoose 'mang the heather'. 'It's oh but I'm longing for my ain folk'. 'Speed the day when I'm on my way to my home in Aberdeen'.

As Scots, we get it both ways, because we love to weep about our lost homeland, and we also like to get away from it so that we can weep in comfort. Even inside Scotland, we like to get away, and the Scot can get away easily because the scale of the country means that no town or city is very far from the ocean. It is possible that the Scots invented the principle of working-class travel because the development of steam-ships virtually forced Glaswegians to visit the beautiful waters of the Firth of Clyde, and they have never lost the habit of travel. Nowadays, they tend to prefer

48

Majorca, where they can learn exotic dances and enjoy cheap drink, and they leave the Clyde waters to English tourists and the middle classes.

But that is too cynical and snide. Scotland is appreciated by the travelling Scot, because it contains such a stunning variety. Loch Lomond, over-commercialised at the end nearest to Glasgow, is big enough to survive unspoiled (and there's another nostalgic song for you). He has the magic Hebridean islands and the infinitely variable west coast, the bracing east coast, the Grampian and Cairngorm mountains and the gentle feminine lands of the south and the Border country. He is richly blessed, and even if he doesn't happen to have visited the Hebrides, he likes the idea that they are there, and takes personal credit for their presence.

HIGHLY PARTICULAR PEOPLE At home, no matter how often the Scot sings about cottages among the heather, he almost certainly lives in a city where heather never grew, and until recently he probably lived in a tenement. There are still plenty of these to be seen, although some early examples have been bulldozed or have simply given up and collapsed. The tenement and the tenement close have made their deep mark on the character of the urban Scot, and this is worthy of some examination.

The traditional Glasgow tenement is three or four storeys high, faced in stone at the front and brick at the back. It is often built in a rectangle, enclosing the backyard or back court. At intervals along its length it is penetrated by a close, or entry, which runs right through from front to back with a slight side-step in the middle where the stone staircase runs to the upper flats. The close, then, is designed as a simple architectural function. Instead, it becomes everything the Glaswegian asks of it. It is a children's playground, it is a refuge for courting couples with no warmer place to go, it is a training area for minor delinquency. Children traditionally learn to subvert organised society by ringing doorbells in closes and running away. The more creative find a piece of rope and tie two facing doors together by the handles before ringing the bells.

A homecoming child at night signals his approach by standing in the close and crying "O-pen, P.N." before he dashes upstairs. This is not from mere high spirits or cussedness. He is anxious to have the door open for him in advance because he knows that foul fiends inhabit the back courts at night and are likely to pursue small boys upstairs and snatch them if their escape route is closed.

In daylight, the back courts too are playgrounds, well adapted to marbles games and feats of derring-do over and along the dividing walls and on wash-house roofs. In practice they are also safe, since a vulnerable child playing in a back court is under the eyes of all the neighbouring housewives at their kitchen sinks. The houses or flats above any close form a community which is close-knit and private at the same time, because a family with its door closed is in its little castle, but with neighbours convenient in moments of sociability or crisis.

The Scottish urchin, and especially in the west, grows up in a world of closes which he knows as a Sherpa knows his mountains. It is unreliably reported that when the Romans came to Glasgow they had to abandon the city because the natives employed a form of warfare which was totally unfair. As the legions marched along the streets in phalanx formation, ready to trample over opposition, there was no opposition to trample. Instead, an undersized native would occa-

50

sionally dash from a close, disable several legionaries with a razor or broken bottle, and then dash back into the close and vanish. The tenement and the close have bred a nation of tough survivors. They had to be tough to survive in the first place.

The product of the varied Scottish environments— the tenement, the crofts, the uplands, the sea-coasts—tends to be both hard and kindly, because a tough environment teaches the necessity of compassion. He is also egalitarian and believes in fair play. The Scot, too, has a passion and a reverence for learning. Universal education was pioneered in Scotland, quite early in the game, by John Knox, who inspired the creation of schools for the lowest orders, sometimes called the ragged schools. The Scottish tradition was that every child should be able to read, write and calculate, and generations of Scots accepted the schoolmaster or dominie as a key figure in society. To become a dominie was the automatic ambition of a capable child.

The hunger for learning was particularly strong in the Highlands, and any family sacrifice was justified. The legendary Highland student (it is not certain that he actually existed) travelled to university in the south with a sack of oatmeal and a barrel of salt herring to keep him going throughout the session, and emerged as a schoolmaster or a minister absolutely crammed with knowledge, and bursting at the seams with porridge and fish. The effect on the population was a high degree of social mobility before that was fashionable, and if you scratch a Scottish professor you are likely to find peasant or artisan blood spurting from the wound.

The tradition has been eroded slightly by changing social conditions which have affected education all over the Western world. All the same, a stranger should avoid classifying any individual Scot too glibly as a simple working man. He is quite likely to have an unsuspected store of learning as well as wit, and he has an unerring instinct for pretentiousness in other people. Nothing can deflate a boaster more brutally than the Scot's laconic comment, "Aye, that'll be right."

Egalitarian, élitist, hardnosed, soft-hearted, clannish and congenial, moralistic and indulgent, the Scots can be downright exasperating. Perhaps other people can display the same paradoxes, but the Scots do it, as they do everything, to extremes. Even their apathy is vigorous and excessive. They are—and in the end I do believe it—highly particular.

In a word, they are very Scots.

Reading List

It sometimes seems that there are as many books written about Scotland and the Scots as there are Scots, and a complete list of suggested reading might well be longer than this small book itself. We may take it for granted that the interested inquirer will find the poems of Robert Burns and the novels of Sir Walter Scott.

For a daunting canon of publications he may consult the Scottish office of the National Book League at 1121 Paisley Road West, Glasgow. The following list is arbitrarily chosen.

Anatomy of Scotland, James McMillan (Leslie Frewin, 1969).

Ane Satyre of the Thrie Estaits, Sir David Lindsay (Ed. J. Kinsley) (Cassell, 1954).

Another Edinburgh; a living guide (Ed. Bill Campbell) (Edinburgh University Student Publications, 1976).

Chambers' Scots Dictionary, Alexander Warrack (W. & R. Chambers, 1952).

The Clans and Tartans of Scotland, Robert Bain (Re-ed by M. O. MacDougall) (Collins, 1966).

Clans, Septs, and Regiments of the Scottish Highlands, F. Adam (Rev. by Sir Thomas Innes of Learney) (Johnston & Bacon, Edinburgh, 1965).

The Guid Scots Tongue, David Murison (Blackwood, 1977).

The Heart of Glasgow, Jack House (Hutchinson, 1965).

The Highland Clearances, John Prebble (Secker & Warburg, 1963).

Highland Costume, J. Telfer Dunbar (Blackwood, 1977).

A History of Scotland, R. L. Mackie (Penguin Books, 1964).

Mary, Queen of Scots, Sir Arthur MacNalty (Johnson, 1960).

Morning Tide, Neil Gunn (Souvenir Press, 1975).

A New History of Scotland, Dickinson and Pryde (Nelson, 1962).

The Paradox of Scottish Culture, David Daiches (Oxford University Press, 1964).

Poems, William Dunbar (Ed. J. Kinsley) (Clarendon Press, 1958).

Poems, Robert Henryson (Ed. C. Elliot) (Clarendon Press, 1963).

The Prehistoric Peoples of Scotland (Ed. S. Piggott) (Routledge & Kegan Paul, 1962).

Robert the Bruce, G. W. S. Barrow (Eyre & Spottiswoode, 1965).

Robert the Bruce, Nigel Tranter (Hodder & Stoughton, 1969-71, and Coronet Books).

Scotland, an Anthology (Comp. Maurice Lindsay) (Robert Hale, 1974).

The Scots Overseas, Gordon Donaldson (Robert Hale, 1966).

The Scots Poems, Robert Fergusson (Ed. J. Telfer) (Scottish Features, 1948).

A Scots Quair, Lewis Grassic Gibbon (Hutchinson, 1946, and Pan Books).

The Scottish National Dictionary (in 10 vols), Grant & Murison (Scottish National Dictionary Association, 1929-76).

The Scottish Political System, James G. Kellas (Cambridge University Press, 1975).

The Second City, C. A. Oakley (Blackie, 1967).

The Shell Guide to Scotland, Moray McLaren (Ebury Press, 2nd edn. 1977).

A Skinful of Scotch, Clifford Hanley (Hutchinson, 1965, and White Lion, 1977).

R. L. Stevenson, a selection and commentary (Ed. M. R. Ridley) (Oxford University Press, 1953).

The Strange Case of Deacon Brodie, Forbes Bramble (Hamish Hamilton, 1975).

The Trial of Patrick Sellar, Ian Grimble (Routledge & Kegan Paul, 1962).

The Wallace, Nigel Tranter (Hodder & Stoughton, 1975, and Coronet Books).

We'll Support You Evermore (Eds Archer and Royle) (Souvenir Press, 1976).

The Wisest Fool (a novel of James VI), Nigel Tranter (Hodder & Stoughton, 1974, and Coronet Books).